StockcarToons 2

More Grins and Spins on the Winston Cup Circuit

by
Mike Smith

Sports Publishing, LLC
www.sportspublishing.llc.com

Director of Production: Susan M. Moyer
Project Manager: Jim Henehan
Developmental Editor: Lynnette Bogard
Cover Design: Kenneth O'Brien

ISBN: 1-58261-610-8

Sports Publishing, L.L.C.
www.sportspublishingllc.com

To Julie, Morgan and Lexie

Foreword . . .

Like most of you, I grew up on comic strips. From Peanuts to Pogo, Prince Valiant to Dick Tracy, I read them all, daily and Sunday. Once I grew old enough to appreciate more of the newspaper than the comics and the ball scores, I became aware and appreciative of Herblock, MacNelly, and the art and wit of the editorial cartoon.

Gasoline Alley was the granddaddy of car-related cartoons. Hot Rodding sported Stroker McGurk, Ed "Big Daddy" Roth and Dave Deal. An all-illustration magazine *Car-Toons* even had a brief run.

Four decades of Tom Wojahn cartoons feature everyday racers: long on ambition, but often short of talent, ingenuity, preparation or funds. And why not? What fun are drivers who win?

It took Mike Smith to answer that question. Smith is the first artist to take the sharp point of the editorial cartoonist's pen and apply it to major-league stock car racing.

I was delighted to discover Mike's work in the daily *Sun* when the NASCAR Winston Cup Series made its first visit to Las Vegas. While I wondered if our sport was funny enough to support a weekly cartoon, he has not suffered for lack of material.

Smith draws his cars and the sport accurately and names the biggest of names. No one in racing is immune. Every driver, car owner, sponsor, crew chief, official, broadcaster, race fan or NASCAR executive is likely to find himself a target of Mike's pointed yet humorous view of the sport.

My favorite StockcarToon shows us a race fan's living room, filled to overflowing with his favorite driver's souvenirs. I'm sure you know someone with a room just like it. But this fan is Mother Nature, and you understand at a glance how Jeff Burton won that string of rain-shortened races.

Mike Smith is a great talent. I'm proud to be a big fan.

Mike Joy
FOX Sports
January 2003

This foreword is dedicated to the memory of sportscar-toonist Joe DeLuca,
one of the heroes onboard Flight 93, September 11, 2001.

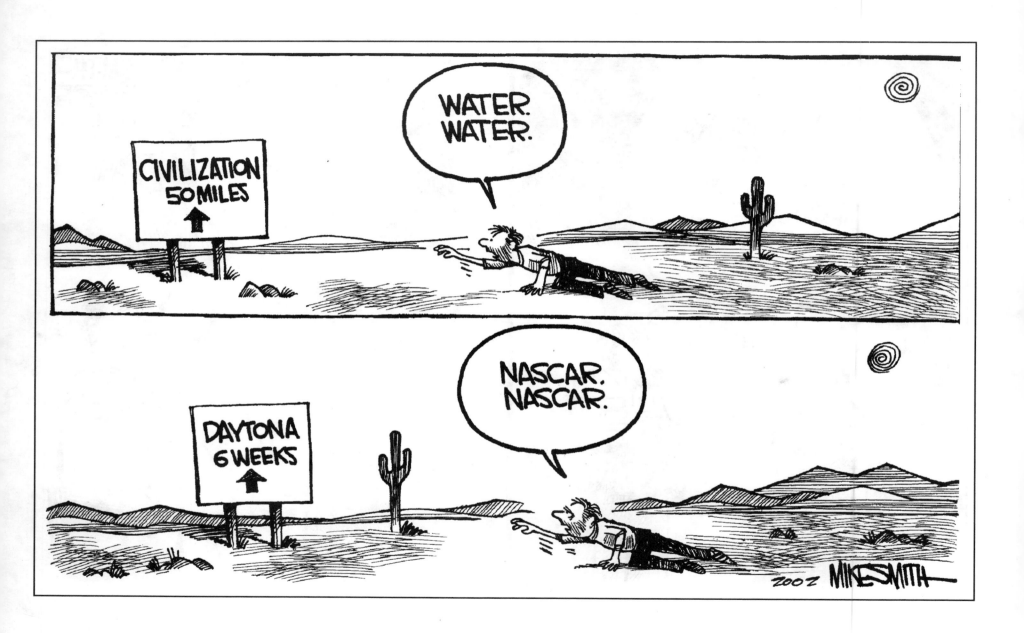

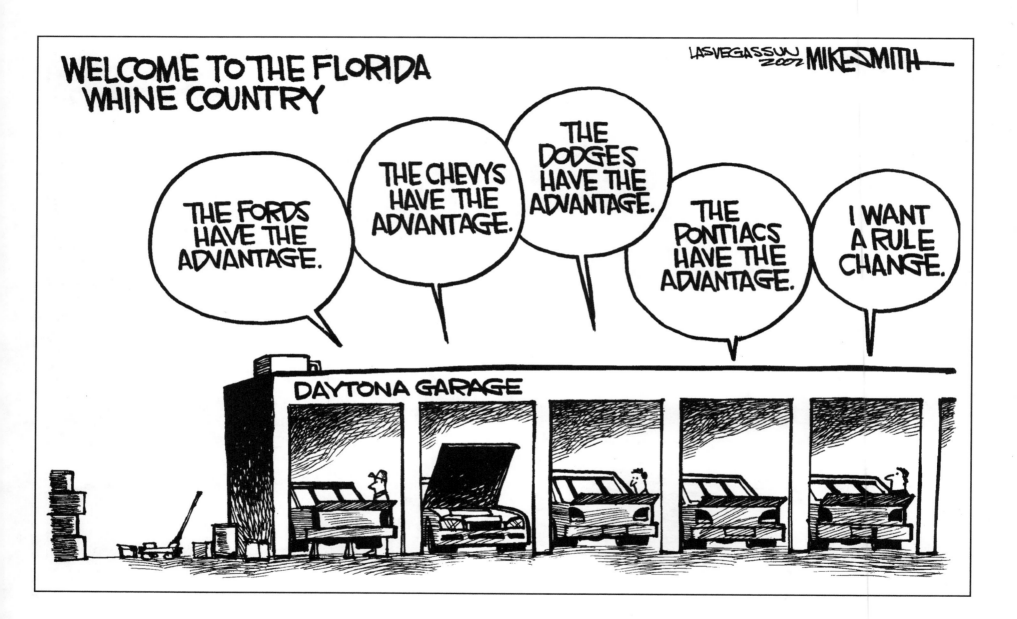

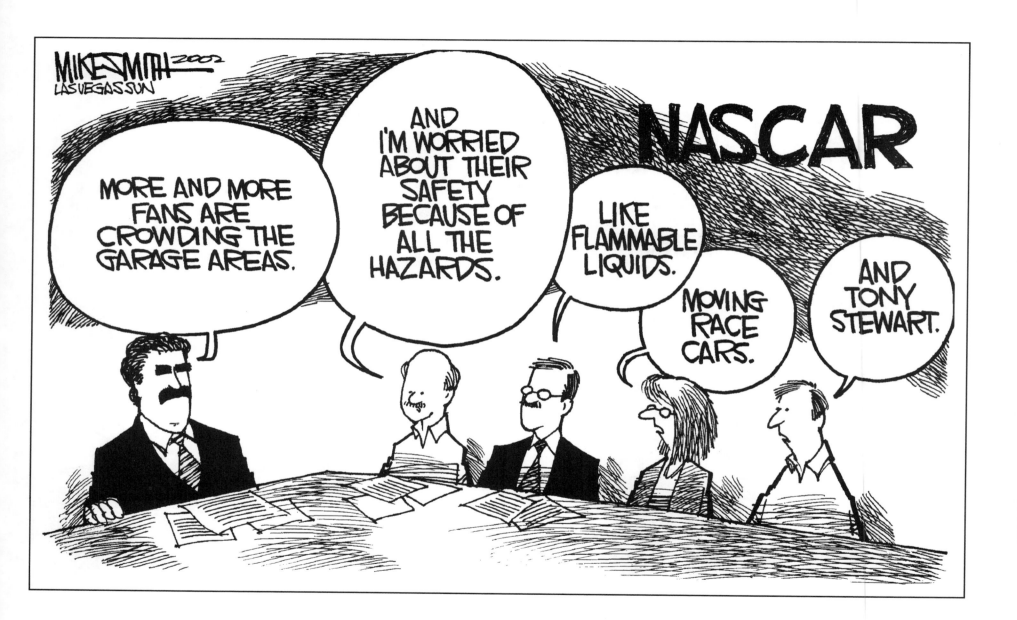

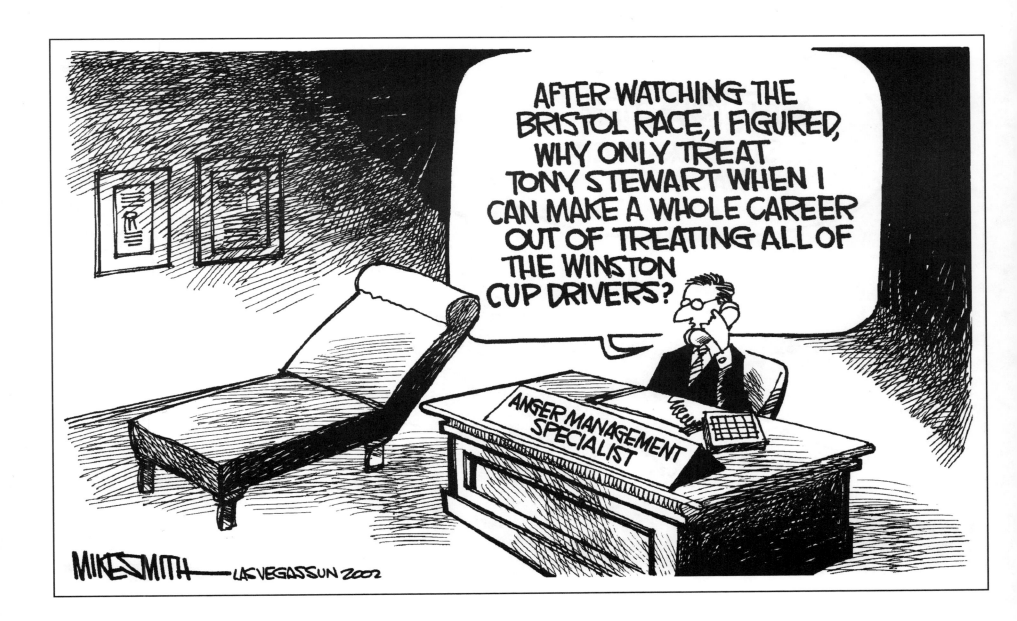

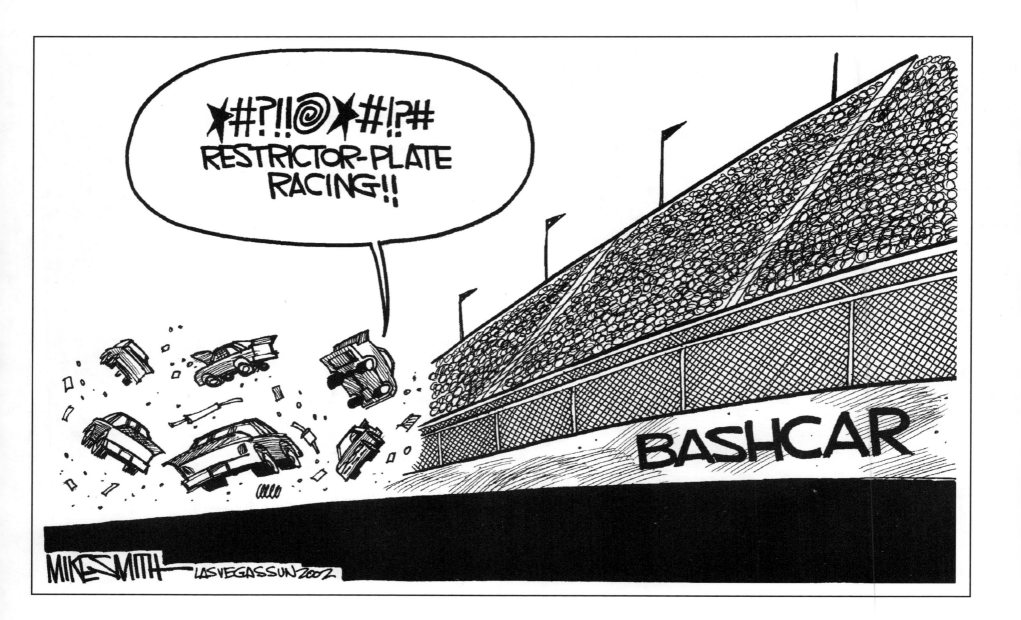

LASVEGASSUN 2003 MIKESMITH
I'VE GOT JUST ABOUT EVERY DIE-CAST CAR THERE IS. SO, I FIGURED WITH A LITTLE PAINT, I COULD HAVE THE REAL THING.
HAROLD, IT'S A HYUNDAI.
8
BUDWEISER

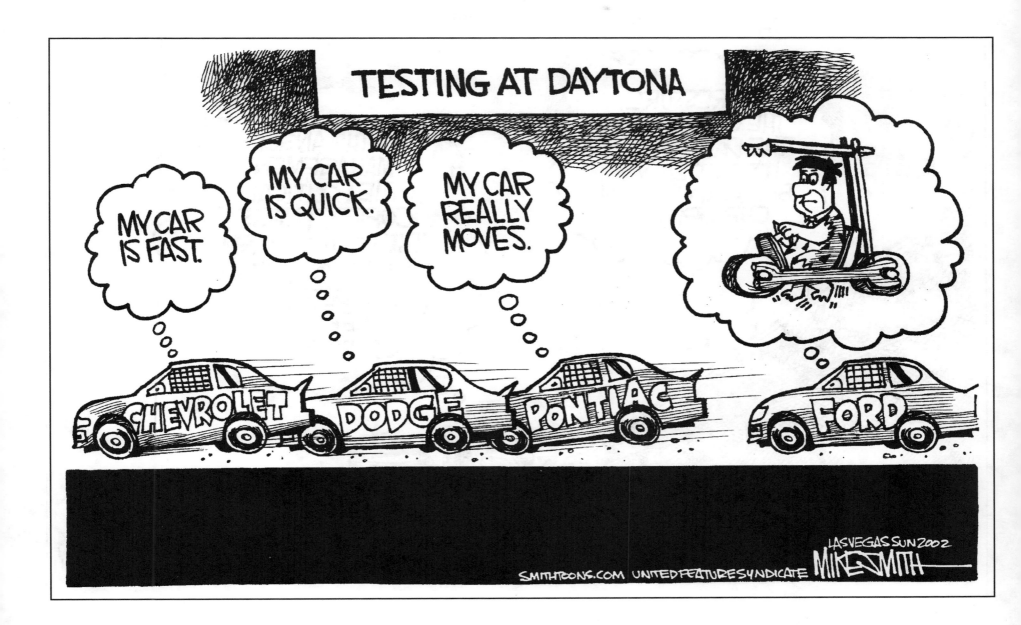

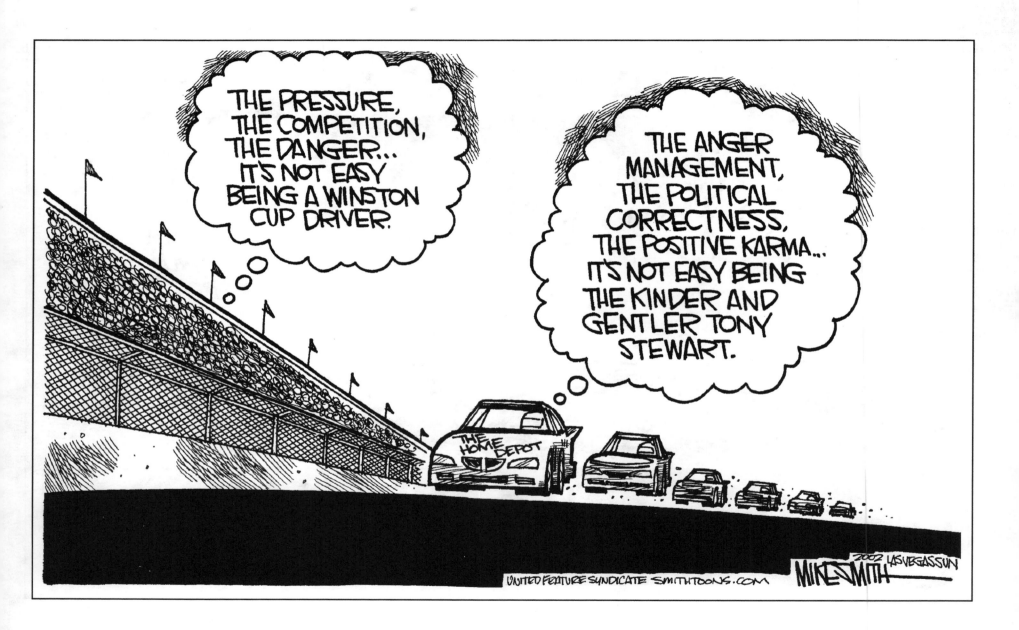

PREPARATIONS FOR THE DAYTONA 500 CONTINUE
OK, LET'S SEE IF WE CAN DO THIS PRACTICE PIT STOP IN 14 SECONDS FLAT.
OK, LET'S SEE IF YOU CAN NAME ALL OF THESE SPONSORS IN 14 SECONDS FLAT.
WINSTON CUP DRIVER
2002 WINSTON CUP SCENE
SMITHTOONS.COM
MIKE SMITH

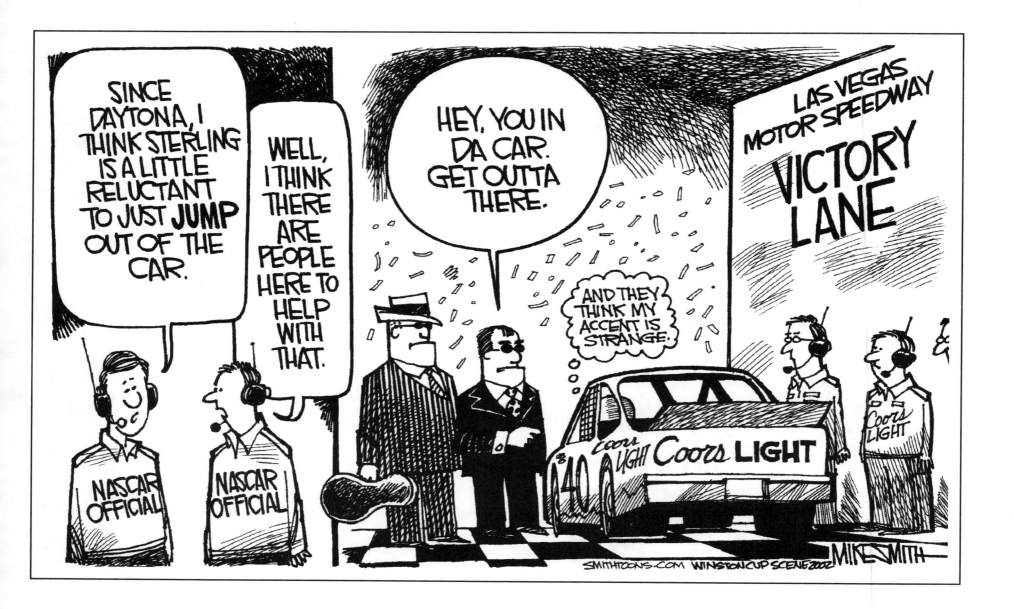

BEFORE KEVIN HARVICK AND ROBBY GORDON...

AFTER KEVIN HARVICK AND ROBBY GORDON...

LASVEGASSUN2002
SMITHTOONS.COM
MIKE SMITH
THE CARS RUN SO RIDICULOUSLY CLOSE AT A RESTRICTOR-PLATE RACE THAT ANY LITTLE THING A DRIVER DOES CAN RESULT IN A WRECK.
ACHOO!
SPIN
SCREECH
CRASH
CRUNCH

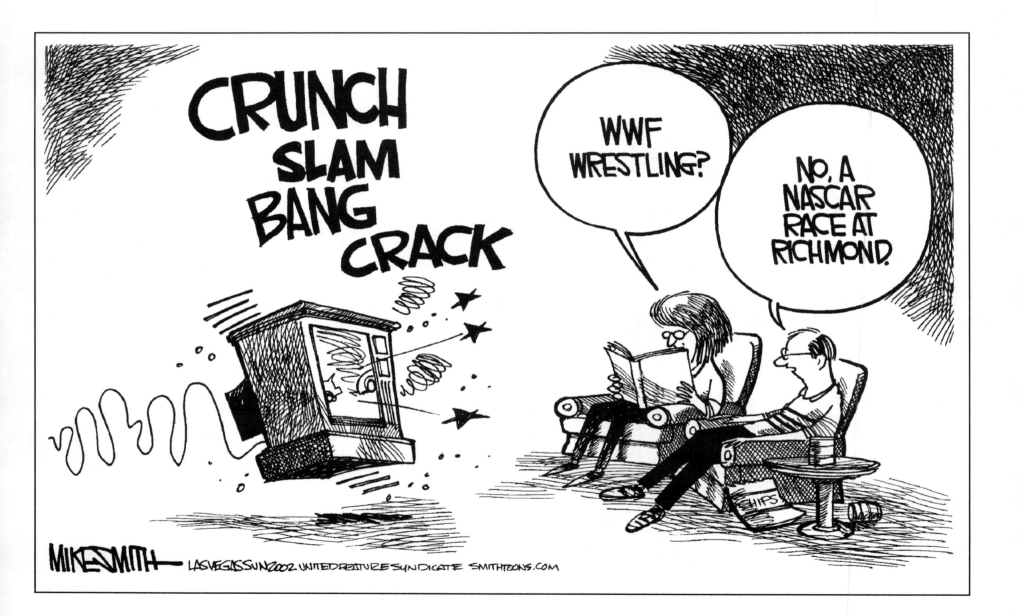

AFTER THE WINSTON, NASCAR DECIDED TO MAKE SOME RULE CHANGES.

THE HELMET TOSS WILL BE BANNED AS A NASCAR EVENT.

#?!@#
RYAN NEWMAN!

MOTORCRAFT

THERE WILL BE A NEW ADDITION TO THE NASCAR TRAILER.

NASCAR

MIKE HELTON IS IN

ANGER MANAGEMENT

THE THERAPIST IS IN

← DRIVERS' ENTRANCE

RESTRICTOR PLATES WILL BE REQUIRED ON ALL SQUEEGEES.

IT KEEPS THE SQUEEGEE FROM SEPARATING FROM THE POLE.

DUPONT

WINSTON CUP SCENE   MIKE SMITH

AND STERLING MARLIN'S CAR WILL BE REQUIRED TO HAVE TURN SIGNALS.

WHAT THE...?

Coors

CAT

2002 SMITHTOONS.COM

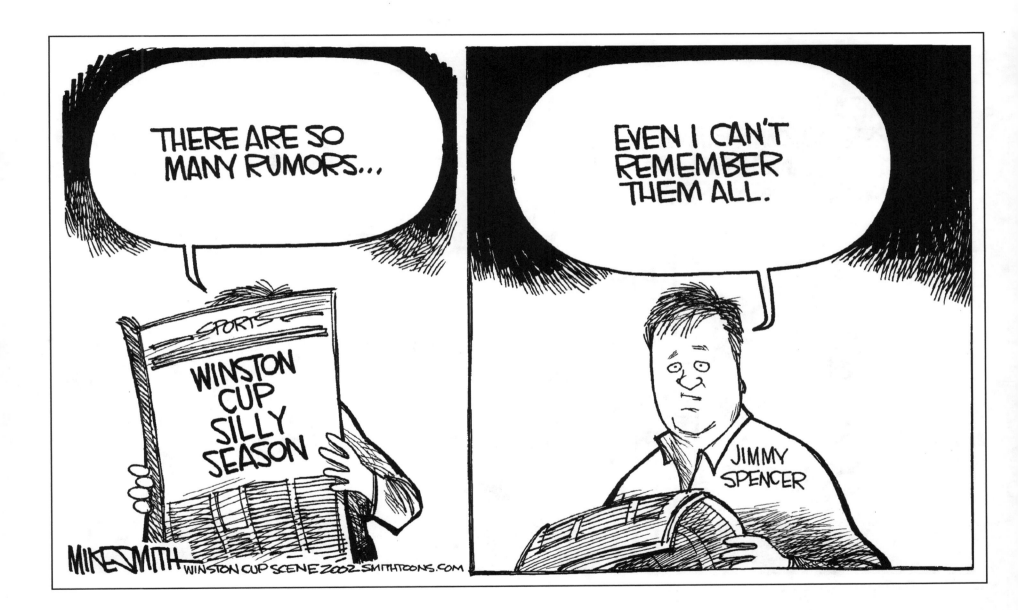

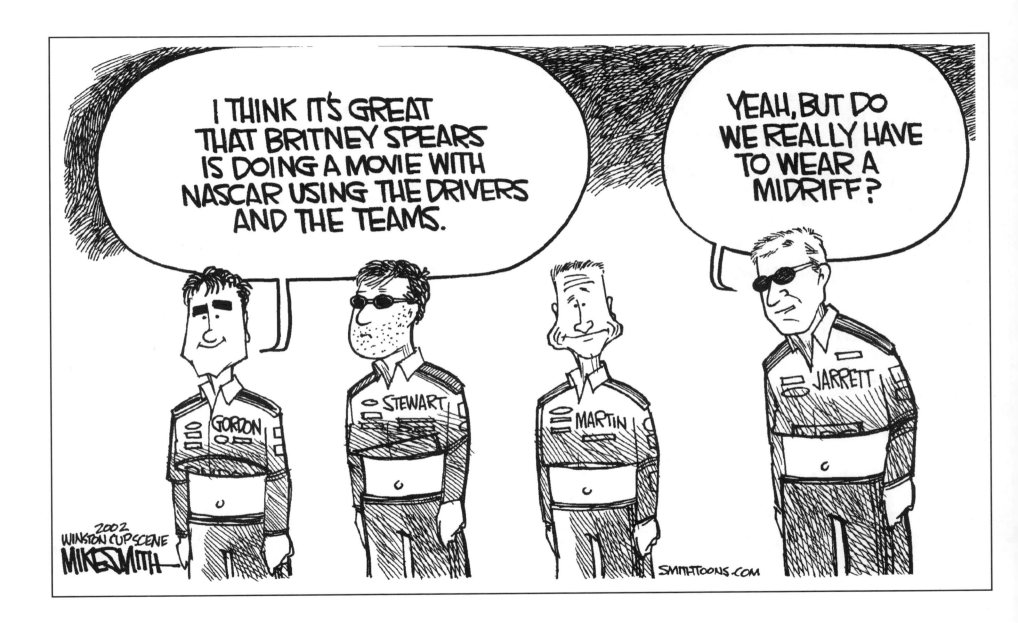

MIKE SMITH LAS VEGAS SUN 2002 UNITED FEATURE SYNDICATE
SMITHTOONS.COM
THEATER
A NASCAR MOVIE
STARRING
BRITNEY SPEARS
HOW MANY DEGREES OF BANKING IS THAT?
ARE YOU TALKING ABOUT THE RACE TRACK OR THE DANCE MOVES?

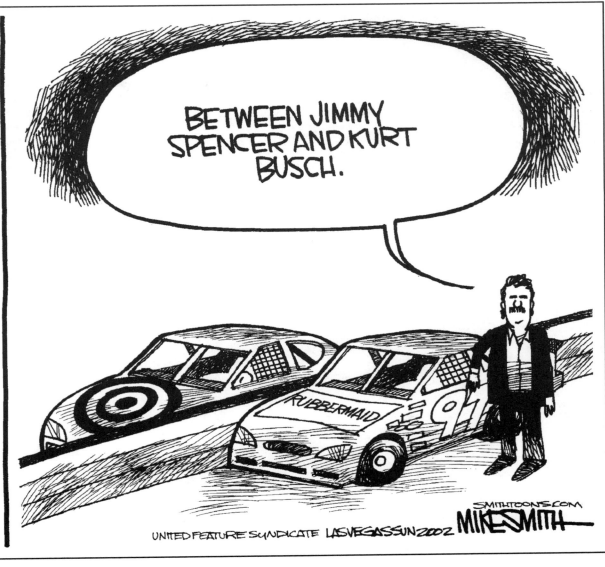

* UNLESS, OF COURSE, WE CHOOSE TO CHANGE OUR MINDS DUE TO RACE LENGTH, RACE CONDITIONS, TRACK TEMPERATURE, AIR TEMPERATURE, TIME ZONES, AREA CODES, ZIP CODES, TIDE MOVEMENTS, FULL MOON, MOOD SWINGS, GLOBAL WARMING, SNOWFALL, CLOUD COVER, BIRD MIGRATION...

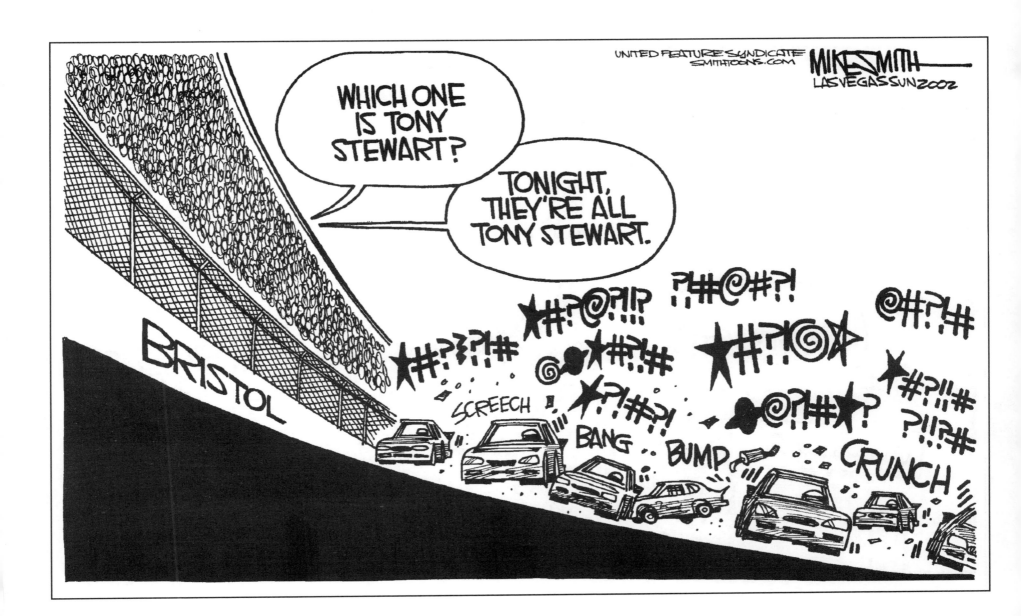

KNOW YOUR NASCAR FANS

DALE EARNHARDT JR.

TONY STEWART

MATT KENSETH

RYAN NEWMAN

RAIN HELPS NEWMAN GET FIRST WIN

StockcarToons 2   97

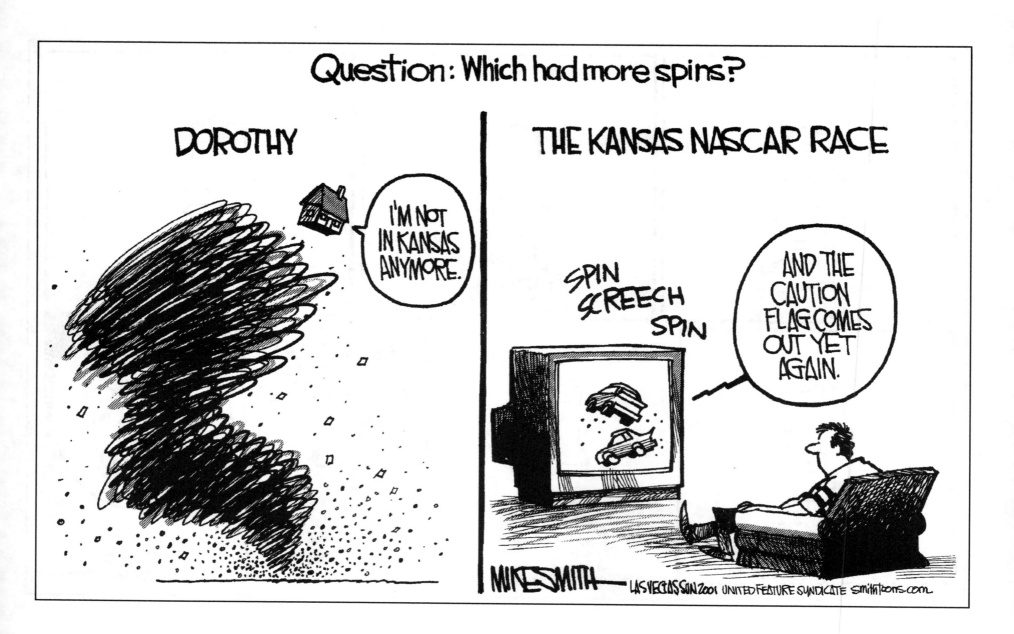

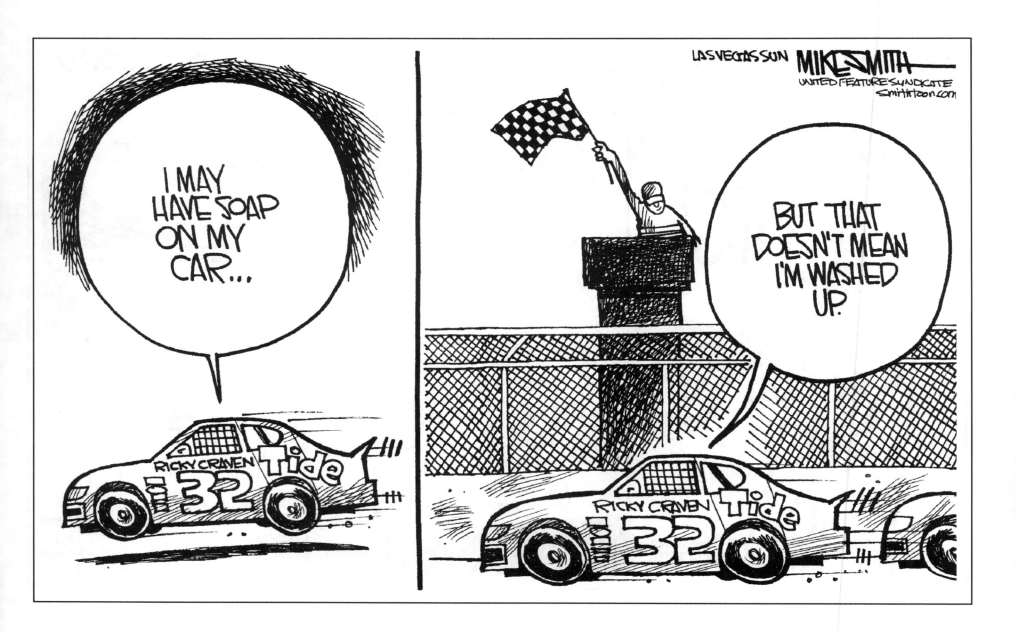

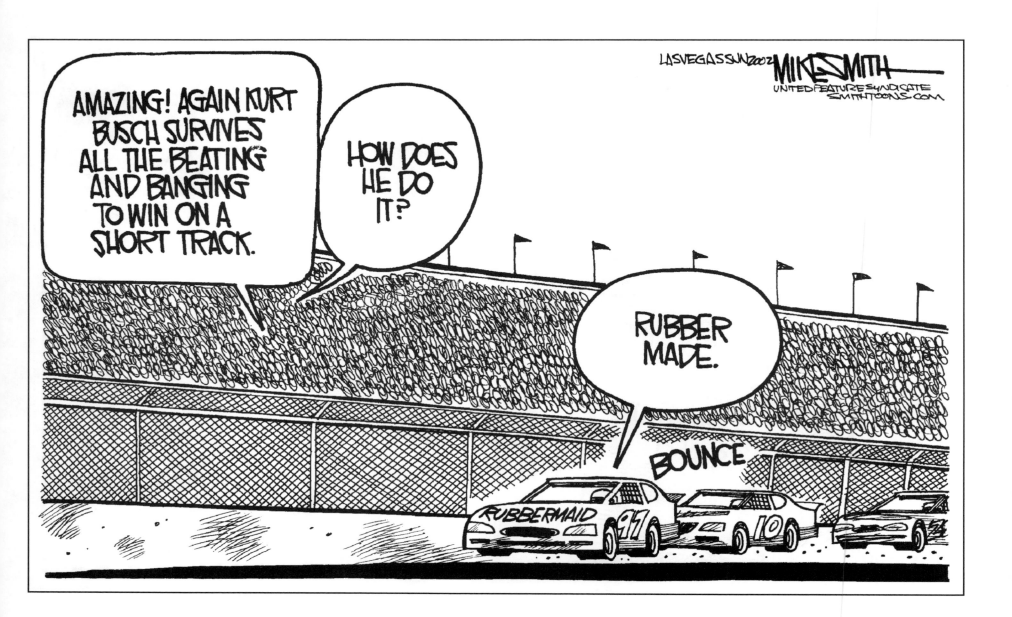

TONY STEWART'S ANGER MANAGEMENT TEAM.

TONY STEWART'S ANGER MANAGEMENT TEAM IF HE LOSES THE CHAMPIONSHIP.

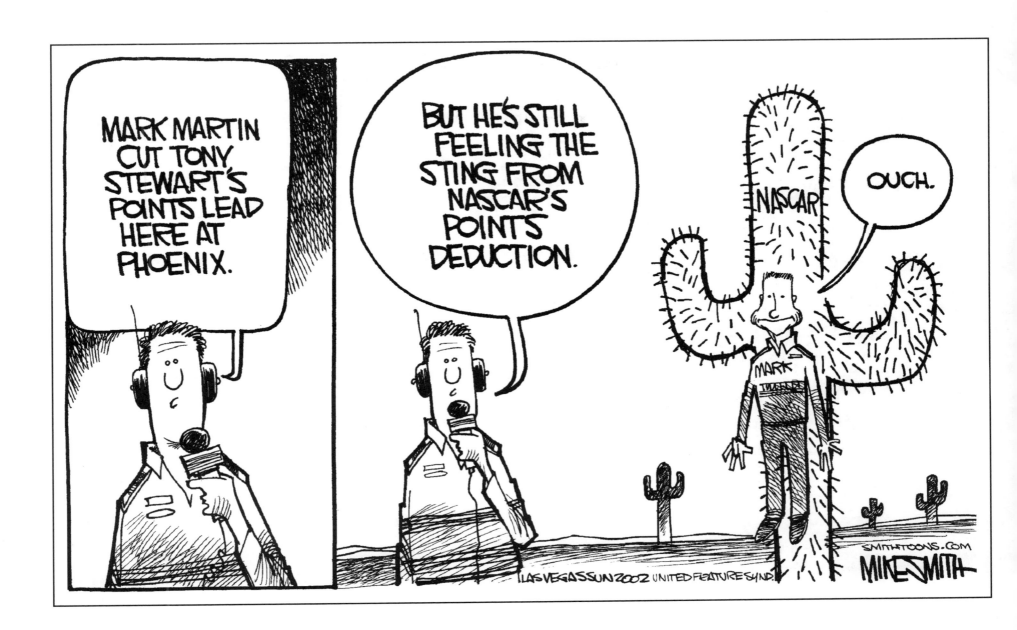

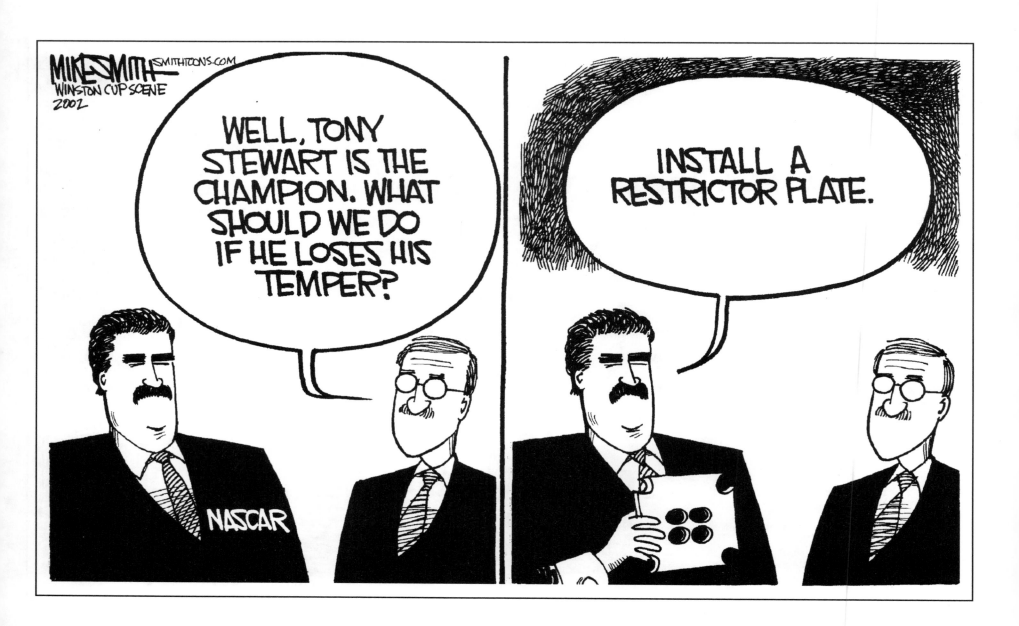

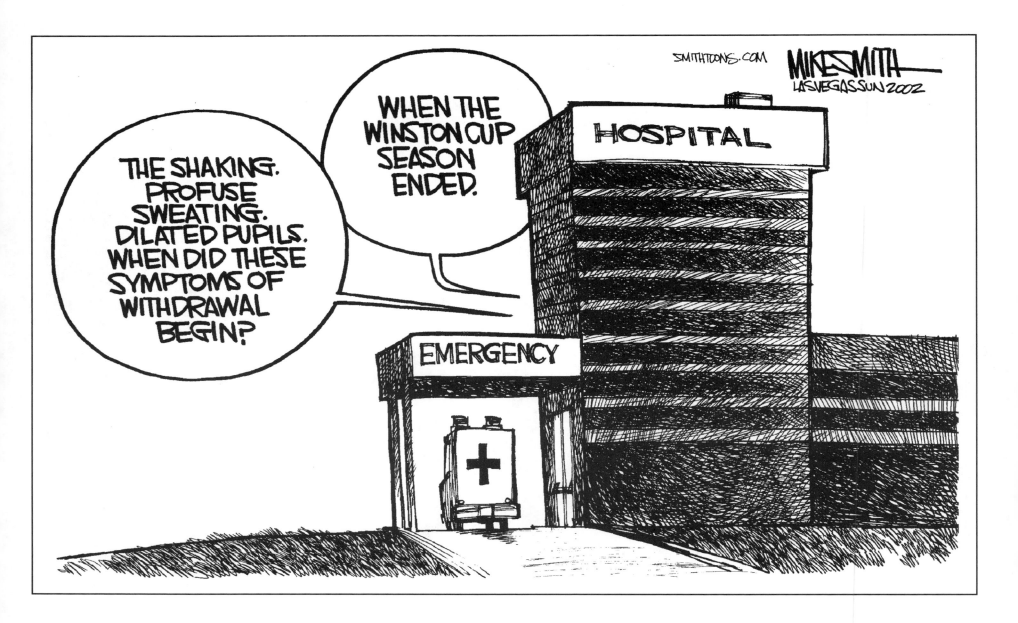

About the Author . . .

Mike Smith is a California native who moved to Las Vegas, Nevada in 1983 to become the staff editorial cartoonist for *The Las Vegas Sun*. In 1998, on a suggestion from his wife Julie, Mike decided to combine his interest in Winston Cup Racing with his love for cartooning to produce *StockcarToons*. Currently, Mike draws a racing cartoon each week for *The Las Vegas Sun* and for *Winston Cup Scene*. Mike's work is syndicated by United Feature Syndicate and he also draws an editorial cartoon each Thursday for *USA Today*.